BEFORE YOU BUY INSURANCE!

Four top Secrets no insurance company or agent will tell you!

By

Ramona R. Taylor

TABLE OF CONTENT

INTRODUCTION

Hey, you made the best decision reading this book. This book is dedicated to the common person who has little or no knowledge about insurance. It's dedicated to all who have suffered in one way or another losing money due to ignorance of some key principles in insurance.

This masterpiece in your hand is more than an equalizer. It will Put you several steps ahead of insurance companies and agents in terms of information, as it seeks to give the common person all the information that is required to win big in insurance!

After reading this book, it would be almost impossible to be taken advantage of by any insurance agent or company or to lose out in insurance!

Insurance is a powerful system that has sadly been abused over the years, due to a very serious and common problem which is IGNORANCE!

This book will explain why some people lose money invested in insurance. Knowledge they say is power and when knowledge about any subject is lacking, there are bound to be problems.

At the end of this book, you will be practically armed with every bit of information you need regarding insurance.

Every information shared in this book is universal and can be universally applied. I assure you that after reading this book, you will never make any mistakes in insurance.

CHAPTER 1

WHAT INSURANCE IS

INSURANCE IS A LEGAL CONTRACT:
Insurance is a legal agreement between two parties where one party, (the insurance company) agrees to compensate the other party when a specific event which is stated and known by both parties at the beginning occurs.

This compensation is based on prompt and regular payment of an agreed amount called **premium** by the insured. There is an important principle in insurance that states "no premium no cover" Payment of Premium is what qualifies the insured to be compensated in the occurrence of any event spelt out from the beginning e.g fire outbreak, theft, accident, or death. Hence payment of premium should be taken seriously by the insured. And because it is a legal agreement, it is legally binding on both parties. Meaning that both parties can be held responsible for a bridge in the contract.

Before we move further, I would like to define some major terms you would encounter in the insurance sector.

1. INSURER: This term refers to the insurance company that agrees to pay an agreed compensation in the when a specified event occurs.

2. INSURED: The person who applies to be compensated when a specified event occurs and pays a fee known as a premium to activate the contract.

3. PREMIUM: An amount or fee paid by the insured to validate the contract and ensure its continuity.

4. CLAIM: This is the compensation paid by the insurance company to the owner of an insurance policy known as the insured or their beneficiaries as the case may be when a particular event occurs.

5. SUM ASSURED: This is the amount payable In the event of an occurrence listed at the beginning or the amount payable at maturity.

INSURANCE IS RISK MANAGEMENT

Insurance entails managing the risk or uncertainty associated with human life and events. A man who buys a car today runs the risk of losing that car due to an accident, fire outbreak, or theft. If anything happens to that car, He gets to bear the financial burden of fixing the car whether or not he planned for it.

Life is full of unforeseen events and uncertainty, but planning drastically reduces the rate of uncertainty. We will all not live forever and unforeseen events may occur. Insurance is having a plan on the ground even before an unforeseen event happens, in order to drastically reduce and in some cases eliminate the consequences that may arise due to that event.

For example, John takes a health insurance policy knowing that he is human and is liable to fall ill during the year. Now he may or may not fall ill. If he does not, at least he had peace of mind knowing that his hospital expenses for the year would be catered for.

Meanwhile, If he does fall ill, he doesn't need to worry about hospital bills. Chances are that he might get to spend even more than what he paid as a premium. So which is better? Be taken by surprise or plan beforehand?

It therefore is a show of financial intelligence to plan for the future with insurance because you pay less and get more. Usually, the premium paid is nothing compared to the compensation that is given back because everyone who bought that policy has shared the burden.

INSURANCE IS TAKING RESPONSIBILITY

It takes a futuristic person with a deep sense of responsibility to take an insurance policy especially when it comes to life insurance. If you don't feel responsible for anyone and never think about the future, having an insurance policy would not make any sense to you.

Insurance is protecting your finances in the future, so you don't spend unnecessarily when you least expect it. It's also protecting the future of those you love. It is you ensuring that whether you are there or not, your loved ones are well taken care of

INSURANCE IS PLANNING FOR UNFORESEEN EVENTS IN THE FUTURE!
You don't take an insurance policy when an unexpected event has already happened. Then it would be too late. Because you want to be thoughtful and futuristic in your approach, you take an insurance policy when it seems like you don't need it, and it would speak when you need it the most.

INSURANCE IS A COMMON POOL
Insurance is a communal pool or social pool as I like to call it. People Benefit from insurance as a result of other people's contributions in the form of insurance policies, so it is a pool of people's contributions.

For example, If 100 people take an insurance policy for a specific term, not all of them would be affected during that period and make a claim. Those who get affected would be compensated for and from their contribution and the contribution of those who were not affected. So the affected group gets paid from this collective pool.

Therefore, it's wrong to assume that your money is lost or goes back to the insurance company when a particular event does not happen to you. That is not true. Just because you didn't make a claim does not mean someone else did not. If you would gladly help a friend, neighbor, or brother in need you should be able to gladly take an insurance policy. Insurance takes care of events that are not planned for. It could happen to anybody. It could be your turn tomorrow.

You can make all the difference by just buying an insurance policy! You surely would be blessed for it. I have seen cases where people have to donate money when a person passes on, meanwhile, the simplest insurance package would have taken care of all the expenses with just a small premium.

INSURANCE IS AN EQUALIZER BETWEEN THE POOR AND THE RICH.

We live in a world where certain privileges are reserved for super-rich people. Privileges like the best hospitals, the best schools, having a will and leaving an inheritance for children and grandchildren, etc.

The only hope of the common person is insurance. With insurance, the common person can do all the things I listed above. Your salary might not buy you treatment in a standard hospital but a health insurance policy can. With a life insurance policy, you can have a will and leave an inheritance in millions for your children or grandchildren. You can also send your children to the best schools with insurance.

CHAPTER 2

WHAT INSURANCE IS NOT

INSURANCE IS NOT A DOOM SENTENCE:
Many people believe if they take an insurance policy, they are preparing for their death or they are preparing for bad things to happen to them. Insurance has no way of influencing good or bad things happening in your life. It does not determine If you would be involved in a road accident, fire outbreak, or illness. If insurance has any effect then it should be a positive one because of the peace of mind that comes with knowing that you have plans in place for whatever situation that may arise in the nearest future. Even God blesses us more when we think about others rather than ourselves alone.

You can go a full year without experiencing any accident but accidents happen every day and humans like you and I get affected. Your money contributed in the form of a premium helps solve the problem. You might be the one in need of support tomorrow.

2. IT IS NOT A GET RICH QUICK SCHEME:

Insurance seeks to help genuine people, not fraudsters or criminals. Don't take out an insurance policy to be fraudulent or smart. You would lose big time with such an attitude. Insurance seeks to step into genuine cases and better society that is why claims are seriously investigated to ensure that no one is trying to take advantage of the public money pool.

3. IT IS NOT SCAM:

Stop listening to people saying Insurance is a scam. As I said earlier, the major problem is ignorance. There are certain secrets that if you do not know, you would lose your money and that's exactly why this book was created, to eliminate the ignorance on your part. Do not be deceived, people all over the world are benefiting from insurance policies in their millions even right now. and it can be so in your case.

CHAPTER 3

WHY SOME PEOPLE LOSE THEIR MONEY IN INSURANCE

Some people buy insurance but do not get their claims due to the following reasons:

1. LACK OF ATTENTION TO DETAILS:

When taking an insurance policy take note of the following:

NAME: Make sure your name aligns in all your documents including the bank account you would prefer to be paid with.

AGE: make sure you give your correct age and it has to align with whatever document (means of Identification) you are presenting especially when it comes to life insurance.

POLICY NUMBER: This is your policy I.D. number. It's like your account number. Make Sure you include it in the transaction details for every premium payment you make.

POLICY DOCUMENT: This is the proof that you have an existing policy. It also contains all the information you need to know about your policy. You usually have between 15-30 days to process it. A lot of people take their policy documents for granted and that's why they lose.

Take time to go through your document, Ask your insurance agent questions during this period and if you are not satisfied you may opt out. That's why you need an insurance agent that knows their onion well. Keep this document safe and take note of your policy commencement date.

If the insurance company decides to breach the contract, you can take it up with the insurance regulatory body in your country. The policy document which contains the terms and conditions of the plan would be referred to by insurance regulatory bodies. So know what's in your policy document and be ready to exercise your right.

2. IGNORANCE: I consider ignorance to be the major reason why people lose big in insurance. They just buy a policy based on what they are told by a marketing agent without seeking to understand or verify.

People lose in insurance due to ignorance of two things:

i) How insurance works

ii) The insurance plan they have chosen.

When you take an insurance plan, you need to understand when to make payments and what happens if you don't, you need to understand if there's a provision for grace when you skip your payments. You need to know the events that you are covered for, e.g. fire outbreak, accident, critical illness, theft, death, etc. You need to know how long you would be covered and the benefits of that plan.

CHAPTER 4

FOUR TOP SECRETS NO INSURANCE COMPANY OR AGENT WOULD TELL YOU!

Before you ever take an insurance policy you must know the following secrets.

1. **There are principles guiding insurance and when you break one you lose big time.**

As simple as this sounds, many people don't know this. They think insurance companies just act out of their discretion. It would interest you to note that If any of these principles are broken by the insured then the insurance company is not entitled or liable to pay any claims.

Unfortunately, many people don't know these principles so they tend to break the rules unknowingly and have to suffer for it.

Trust me, I do not want that for you, so I would mention the 6 principles of insurance and explain in simple terms four out of these six powerful principles as they affect the payment of claims.

THE SIX POWERFUL PRINCIPLES OF LIFE INSURANCE

Six (6) principles guide insurance but to keep it simple I will just stick with explaining the four most important as it determines whether you get paid claims or not.

1. Insurable interest
2. Utmost good faith
3. Proximate cause
4. Indemnity
5. Subrogation
6. Contribution

INSURABLE INTEREST

Before you insure someone or something, you have to have the right to do so by ownership, possession, existing relationship e.g family members, mortgagee and mortgagor etc you can't insure your neighbor or your friend or even your fiancee unless you are business partners. A lender can insure a debtor, a wife can insure her husband and vice versa.

UTMOST GOOD FAITH:

I mentioned earlier that insurance is out to help genuine people. So you have to state everything within your knowledge that relates with your life and can influence your making a claim such as nature of work, location, existing health conditions, risky hobbies e.g mountaineering, surfing, car racing, etc.

You have to give every required information without holding back so the insurer can know the degree of risk they are taking on and if they are willing to do so. If it is discovered you withheld any information you were aware of, then you just voided your insurance contract. This is one of the reasons why some people don't get paid claims in insurance. They want to be smart so they conceal information. If it's discovered after investigation that you Lied about your age, health status, or any other information you were required to provide, you might not get paid. For example, You can't start a life insurance policy when you have a terminal disease without telling the insurance company. It is fraudulent!

PROXIMATE CAUSE

This is another very important factor. It is the major cause which can be directly linked to a loss or the occurrence of an event which in this case could be accident, fire outbreak, flood, permanent disability, critical illness or death.

 The insurance company has to investigate to see that a particular loss was not faked and was not caused by deliberate negligence. You can't take an insurance policy that protects your car and then go car racing with the same car. It is a fraud!

Any loss caused by the insured's involvement in illegal activities will not be recognized in insurance. For example, a robber who went to rob and got shot dead will not have his insurance benefits given to his beneficiaries because the cause of his death is illegal.

Also, if someone is drunk while driving, they are responsible for the consequences of that action.

INDEMNITY

This is the no-profit clause in insurance. This principle states that the insured gets compensated only for what was lost. No more no less. It is therefore a show of ignorance to take an insurance policy with two insurance companies on the same car or house and expect to get double payment if there's an eventuality. Both insurance companies would liaise and pay you exactly what you lost. No more than that! This principle is very important as it is the foundation for the other two principles which are contribution and subrogation.

2. The second secret you should know is that Insurance companies don't want you to die or bad things to happen to you: When there's an eventuality, insurance companies have to bear the risk which is usually huge. So they are not happy when something bad happens. Therefore, don't think insurance companies delight in bad occurrences and that they are prophets of doom. Don't allow this mindset to deter you from making appropriate plans for your future and that of your family.

3. You can eliminate the uncertainty or risk associated with insurance.

There's a way to eliminate the uncertainty associated with insurance and be 100 percent sure of getting up to 100% or more return on your investment. I'll tell you this for free! Insurance plans is divided into 2 variations.

- Pure Risk
- Investment

Note that all life Insurance policies be it pure risk or investment have an automatic benefit for your beneficiary. Taking an investment policy in Insurance gives you a life cover automatically.

Pure Insurance plans arc always 50:50. E.g Car, property, Health, life insurance. Meaning that the event you are insuring may or may not occur.

But guess what! only a whole life insurance policy allows you to be sure of 100% of your investment and even more! Not just a life policy but a whole life policy. All other pure risk insurance policies are 50-50 meaning an event may or may not occur. but in a whole life insurance policy, you can be sure that the said event would occur because we all will not be here forever. That's certain. It's not 50-50. The inevitable is a sure event for everybody.

So you know that when you take a whole life plan, your beneficiaries are surely going to get compensated when you are no more there, no matter how long you live. Remember, a good man leaves an inheritance for his children and great-grandchildren.

You can take a whole life insurance policy knowing that your children will certainly reap the harvest Sooner or later and you can be sure of getting up to 100% or more of what you have invested.

4. Life Insurance is a cheap, easy, and profitable way to lay a better financial foundation for your children.

Imagine that your parents left you with a lump sum of money to begin life with, would life be so much easier?? I bet it would. Insurance is one of the cheapest, easiest, and most profitable ways to pass on a wealthy legacy to your children and consequently your grandchildren.

With an insurance policy, you can ensure that your children will never have to drop out of school or suffer whether you are there or not. If we all had an insurance policy, there would be fewer children on the streets, the rate of crime would reduce, and out-of-school children and poverty rates would also reduce.

Taking a life insurance policy does not affect the length of your days in any way. Instead, it might increase your days on earth because of the peace of mind that comes with it. Not having a life insurance policy is a risk in itself. A life insurance policy is the most important insurance policy to have as it has to do with the lives of people, it has to do with your life and the future of the next generation. A life insurance policy ensures that

1. You leave a valuable inheritance for your children that is far beyond what you could have saved in your lifetime with the same amount.

2. Your children never have to drop out of school or be thrown on the streets at a tender age. Your

investment in insurance will speak when you can't speak for them.

Taking a life insurance policy is the smartest thing to do and if you can afford it, a whole life plan is much better.

CHAPTER FIVE

HOW TO WIN BIG IN INSURANCE

- **Pay attention to details:** Read your policy document properly and if possible employ the help of an expert for interpretation which can be your insurance agent. This is a very important tip. Because this is not your area of specialization you might need the help of an insurance agent or broker. Get familiar with the terms and conditions so you can exercise your right where necessary.

- **Don't miss your premium payments**: if you miss a premium payment for any reason, find out how you can get back on your plan. The best way to secure an insurance policy is by making a single payment. It's usually cheaper to pay at once. Making a single payment eliminates the risk of not following through.

- **Take a life insurance policy and do it when you are in your prime**: Most life insurance policies have age limits so the younger you are the better chances you have and the less premium amount you would pay. Also when you are younger, there are fewer health challenges hence the risk is low making your claims process seamless.

- **Take a whole life insurance policy if you can rather than a specific term policy**

The best form of life insurance is the whole life policy that is applicable throughout your life. A whole life plan is an investment for your family where you get up to 100% or more ROI (return on your investment) depending on your age. This is the only form of insurance where the certainty of an event occurring is 100%. This is because everyone would not live forever. a whole life insurance policy ensures that your family gets taken care of, whenever the inevitable happens. Regardless of how old you are when it happens.

The more your investment, the more your returns. This is the best way to create, preserve, and transfer wealth to your children.

CHAPTER SIX

HOW TO KNOW IF YOU NEED A LIFE INSURANCE POLICY

You need an insurance policy if you meet the following criteria.

1. **Humanity:** You must be human. One thing common with all humans is that we make mistakes, we don't have control over certain events and we will all not live forever. Therefore, if you are reading this book, you know you will be here forever, and not just that but you are prepared to always spend whenever there is an unexpected turn of events, Then you don't need a life insurance policy you should be able to take care of yourself. I urge you to skip this.

2. **You must have dependants:** If you don't have anyone depending on you directly or indirectly for their survival then you might not

need a pure life insurance plan. Although you can take it as a means of leaving an inheritance for your children and grandchildren.

In Summary, if you are human, and you have people dependent on you for survival, or you want to ease the financial burden whenever an unforeseen event happens, ease other people's burden or even prepare towards a future event in your life such as your children's University Education, retirement, investment goals etc. then you need an insurance policy.

CHAPTER SEVEN

HOW TO GET PAID IN LIFE INSURANCE

Documents required for claims processing:

1. Policy document or insurance certificate
2. Claims or liquidation form: you are required to fill out a claims form.
3. Evidence of the occurrence of the said event e.g. pictures of the damaged car, or property. Copy of death certificate, etc
4. Means of identification to ascertain the identity of the person making the claim.
5. A Utility bill is required to authenticate your address.

N/B The earlier a claim is reported the better so every proof required can

be gotten easily and promptly.

HOW TO PROCESS CLAIMS (STEPS)

1. Contact your insurance company either physically or via mail or website

2. Fill a claims form

3. Provide all the requirements, e.g. Pictures, death certificate, medical record, I.D card, etc.

FACTORS THAT DELAY OR PREVENT PAYMENT OF CLAIMS

1. Lack of alignment of name or age

2. Failure to provide required documents

3. When any of the principles of insurance have been broken.

4. When there's a default in payment of premium. Remember no premium, no cover.

CHAPTER 8

HOW NOT TO GET CAJOLED OR COERCED BY INSURANCE AGENTS

The easiest way to avoid this situation is by getting informed! If you have gotten to this point, it means at least you have achieved 80% awareness. From experience I have realized that it's easier to get more information when you go find it out yourself than waiting for it to come meet you. So do your research.

Look at the thriving insurance companies, find out about the product you are interested in, get all the options, and make a choice. choose the one that best suits your needs.

Don't let insurance agents look for you. Look for them so you can have the chance to ask as many questions as possible. You are the one who needs insurance and gets to benefit from an insurance policy. It's about you not about them. So be in control and that's what reading this book has done for you. It has placed you in an informed position.

BONUS EXTRA

Questions you should ask an insurance agent about any plan they're introducing to you.

1. What is the policy term? Find out how long the plan covers you (I advise you go for a whole life plan preferably or a plan that covers your active life)
2. What is the grace period in the case of a missed payment
3. What are the eventualities that are covered? e.g critical illness,
4. Is there a cashback benefit??
5. When will the policy lapse??

How to know a good Insurance company

Transparence is the major trade mark of a good Insurance company. Look out for transparency. Properly spelt out terms and conditions is required.

CONCLUSION

Knowledge they say is power. I believe you have been equipped with everything you need to make an informed decision. I sympathize with you if you have ever lost money investing in insurance. This book was created so it would never happen again and you can regain that which was lost by being in a better informed position.
At this point, if you don't have a life insurance policy, you need to take action now!

If this book has been really helpful to you, please drop a review. The author would love to get your feedback. Keep winning!